Us Teens

Us Teens

written by **Noel .E. Vernon**

illustrated by Niamh Purcell

Nifter Publishing

Us Teens

Author Noel E Vernon Copyright © 2013
Illustrations by Niamh Purcell Copyright © 2013
All rights reserved.

First paperback edition printed 2013 in the United Kingdom
A catalogue record for this book is available from the British Library.
ISBN 978-0-9575934-0-4

Published by Nifter Publishing
For more copies of this book, please go to www.thetaleofus.co.uk

Printed in Great Britain

This book is inspired by and dedicated to **Jonny Baggs**

Who has the capacity to drive me bonkers and make me laugh in equal measures.

Noel
I would like to thank Niamh for her patience and for her
uncanny ability to read my mind, Dana for her poignant
honesty, and finally a special thank you to George for
making life easier for me whilst I wrote this book.
Thank you all I couldn't have done it without you.

Niamh
I would like to thank Noel for giving me a chance, Chris
for hundreds of cups of tea, making my work schedules and
generally being amazing, and finally a big thanks to my family
for all their encouragement.

mustashe pimple.

LAVA
PUS

Contents

It's not fair

It's always me it seems to be
Who does the household chores
Wash the pots and clean your room
Then mop up all the floors
I'm sure me doing all this work
Makes life easier for you
Don't you even realise
I have better things to do
I could go out with all my friends
Or play games on my pc
But no I have to walk the dog
Is this really fair on me
To have no jobs for one whole day
I would pay a million bucks
Though I'm quite sure that won't happen here
Being a teenager really sucks

School Uniform

It's usually black or grey or green
Or sometimes boring blue
No matter what the colour is
It don't look good on you
The ties they almost never match
With our school blazers and yet
They make us look like we have lost
A great big bloody bet
Our PE kit though is far far worse
If we forget it our teacher he rants
We never get away with it though
He makes us do PE in our pants

I HATE HOME WORK

teachers pet.

Teachers

There was stinky O'Rourke
Who would spit when he talked
There was Miss Cheetham
Who looked like an owl
Mr Cook was so think he resembled a pin
Mrs Travis had a permanent scowl
Mr King was so tall
He could see over the wall
At the older kids having a smoke
Miss O'Keefe was quite loud
Mr Timm was so proud
Of the way that he told a joke
Mr Jones was so fat
He would eat this and that
Mrs Turner had huge swollen knees
And Mr Lewis's teeth
When looked at from beneath
Reminded me of some piano keys

4

Timetable

My first lesson today is in room number 6
Way over in block 42
When that's finished it's over to block 7 or 8
Or is it room 14 nobody knew

We then have our lunch and then over again
To block 42 but this time room 4
Next lesson is over in block 26
Does anyone here know the score

We are now in block A in a room called Cadiz
This system is really absurd
I just wish they'd keep the rooms all the same
Instead of using numbers and colours and words

It gets even worse though later today
We're over in a block called maroon
Stephen Hawking would struggle with this oh my God
Home time please be with us real soon

From block yellow to C then to room 53
On block 19 next to block royal blue
If you think you're confused then spare a small thought for us
Just getting around isn't easy to do

My head it now hurts I've gone dizzy as well
Surely it can't be just me
To find your way round this building requires
A first class engineering degree

Passing Notes

What the hell is that she's wearing
Does she really think that's cool
That top together with that skirt
Then wearing them to school
Pass it on to Dana
Then Debs and Tracey too
What decade is she living in
She makes me wanna spew
When you have read it tear it up
Then throw it in the bin
Before that fashionista
Grasses me up to Mrs Flynn

6

Girls stink

When I was nine I thought girls stink
When I was ten I thought girls stink
When I was eleven I thought girls still stink
When I was twelve I thought Phwoooooooar, girls have boobs!

Boys Smell

When I was nine I thought boys smell
When I was ten I thought boys smell
When I was eleven I thought boys still smell
I'm now twenty eight and I think all men are shits.

Under My Bed

There's week old pants and smelly socks
There's lots of fluff there too
There's posters pens and paints and stuff
There's a half full jug of glue
There's a football baseball woollen mitts
There's a scary vampire mask
There's bits of crisps and sticky sweets
There's a tartan thermos flask
There's homework I should have handed in
There's a novel that's been signed
And oh there's a pile of magazines
I don't want my mum to find

Friends

We cannot live without them
When I'm upset they're there for me
I tell them all my secret stuff
That's what friends are for you see

We chat and laugh and talk about
Boys clothes and films and shoes
And if we fancied boys at school
Which one of them we'd choose

One day we will all leave here
All grown up and not so cool
But I always will remember you
My bestest friends from school

Bullies

They would take all my money and most of my lunch
Then punch me and pretend that was cool
If I ever grassed up to a teacher bout this
They would slap me and call me a fool

They would threaten to do all sorts to me like
Shave my hair off then paint my head brown
Then when on the school bus going back to my house
They would strip me and leave me in town

They will spit in my eye and throw my shoes on the roof
Put my kit in the girls changing room
They will smash up my phone and put fireworks in my bag
Then sit back and watch it go boom

I'm just biding my time every dog has its day
Things will turn around one day you'll see
In a few years from now these neanderthal pricks
Will be begging to come work for me

B.O.

I seem to always get them
Sitting next to me
The ones who never seem to wash
And smell a little bit of wee

It's like a mixture between two things
I thinks it's sweat and real old cheese
Can no-one else here smell it
I'm begging help me please

Soap isn't that expensive
Nor deodorant in a stick
He doesn't seem to notice
It's making everyone feel sick

Someone has to tell him
Which person will be bold
But be assured it won't be me
Onto my nose I have to hold

There is always one in every class
Who smells like fresh made poo
If you don't know who your classes is
It may turn out to be you

Homework

We have maths and there's tech and
of course there's RE
Biology chemistry too
History geography then there's IT
Physics French and then loads more to do
Spanish then English both language and lit
German then even more math
I must spend more time on my homework each day

It's driving me mad
Then my big sister spends in the bath
I dont know how much more I can take

Perhaps I'll say that it's lost
Or the dog ate it maybe or Dad threw it out
If I do then I know it will cost
They will probably double
The amount that I get
Is there an end to this unfair endeavour

So' I'll start it tonight
And get on with it or
No doubt I'll be
grounded forever

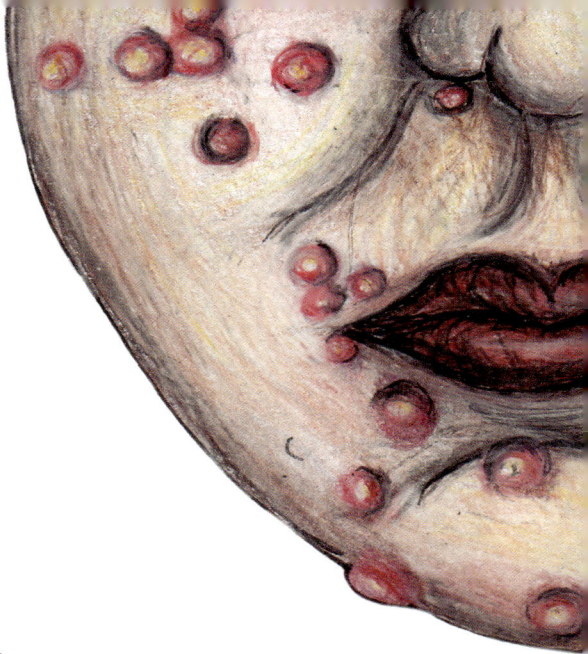

Zits 1

I was warned that soon they will appear
On my chin and on my cheek
And now they're here and gonna spread
The futures looking bleak

My Sisters Best Friend

Does she even notice me I think she's really fine
Those deep blue eyes that soft blond hair
I'm sure she can't wait to be mine
Tonight I'll smooth talk her I'm pretty sure this will work
Although she has got a boyfriend I know
I'll tell her that if she plays her cards right with me
Then I might just become her new beau

That didn't quite work out like I wanted it to
I'm not really that bothered at all
She's doesn't give me the hots and she's covered in spots
Her breath smells and she's too tall
Her conversation is dull and she can't dance very well
On this subject I don't want to linger
Cause I didn't really like her at all anyway
In fact I think she's a dirty old minger

Oh no there he is just staring away he really gives me the creeps
With his mouth open wide does he not have any pride
Eww I bet he dreams of me when he sleeps
He is coming across now what can I do
I think he's gonna ask me out on a date
But he's slimy and sad and looks nothing like Brad
I guess I'll just have to give it him straight

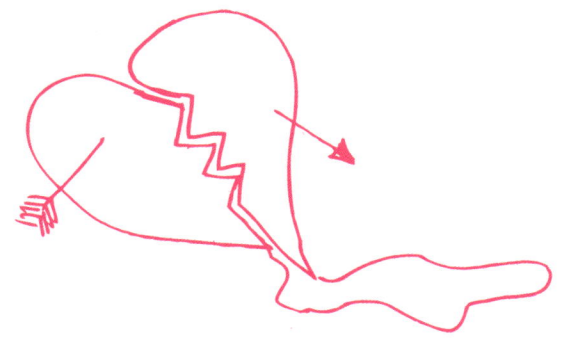

I didn't want to be cruel and when I see him at school
I'll say sorry and tell him the truth
He's not really that bad it's just he isn't my bag
But we all go through this in our youth
I hope that he will understand what I say
If he doesn't then he can stay on the shelf
He has no chance with me and I'd like him to see
That he can always play with himself

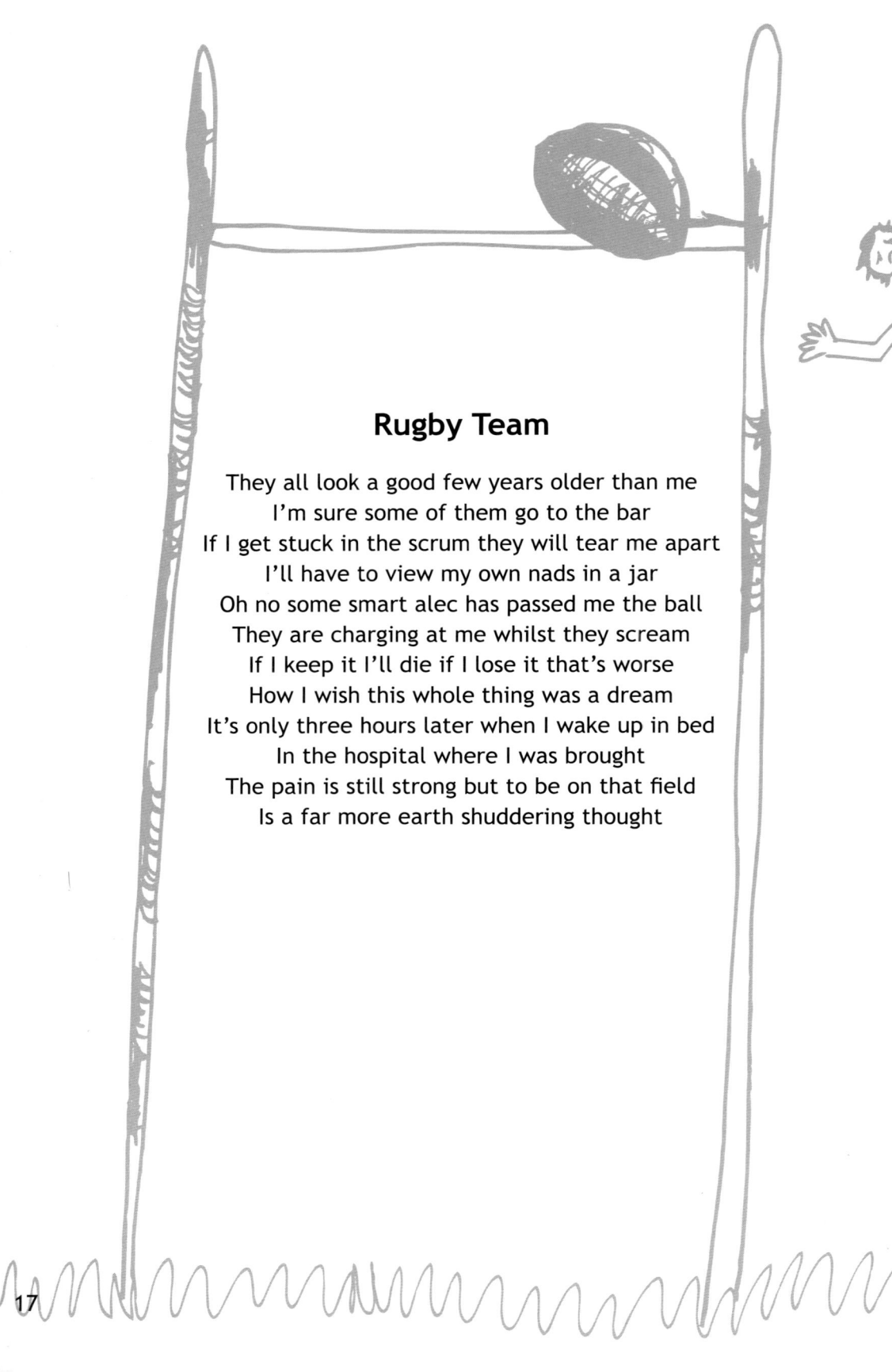

Rugby Team

They all look a good few years older than me
I'm sure some of them go to the bar
If I get stuck in the scrum they will tear me apart
I'll have to view my own nads in a jar
Oh no some smart alec has passed me the ball
They are charging at me whilst they scream
If I keep it I'll die if I lose it that's worse
How I wish this whole thing was a dream
It's only three hours later when I wake up in bed
In the hospital where I was brought
The pain is still strong but to be on that field
Is a far more earth shuddering thought

Texting

School Crush

Shall I ask him out today
I'm so scared that he'll say no
I don't want him to think that I'm uptight
Or even worse a ho
If he say's no I'll die inside
And never show my face
Again around this godforsaken awful hellhole place
But if he says yes and I wish he would
How my heart would sing with glee
That we will go to see a film
My new boyfriend and me

20

Family parties

They come around usually every couple of months
For birthdays and weddings and deaths
We all get together to celebrate stuff
From a first born to someone's last breath

They tend to end up all being the same
Oldies get drunk and the kids nick their fags
Then when all the adults fall asleep in their chairs
We then rifle their pockets and bags

The singing then starts and we all get our turn
Some mumble some shout and some sing
Uncle Frank thinks he's Usher Auntie Pat thinks she's Cher
Cousin Sean thinks he's Elvis the King

At the end of the night there is usually a fight
Over something that happened back when
But no-one will ever hold on to a grudge
Cause we will soon be together again

Zits 2

I've got a date on Saturday
It's now really doomed to fail
When my face starts to resemble
A book written in Braille

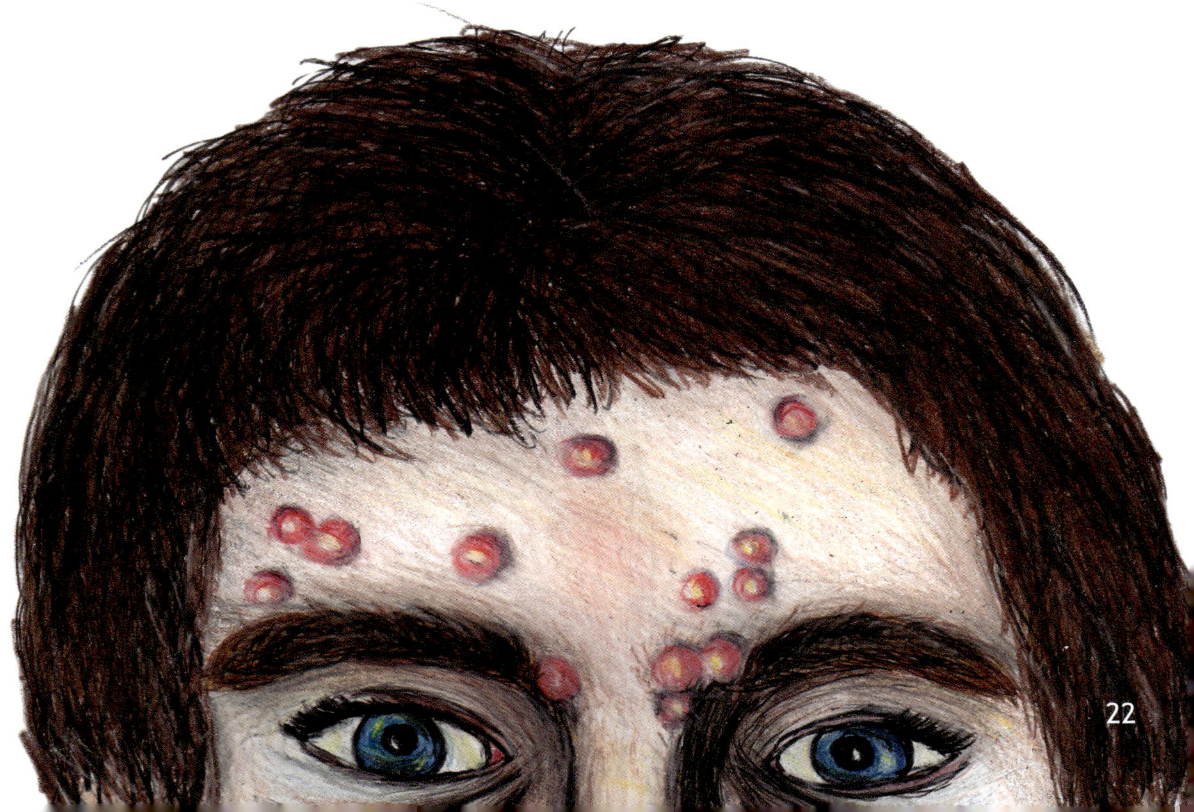

Pets

I have had goldfish more than once
Their names were Flip and Flop
My hamster Sniff was four years old
When it was his time for the chop
He's buried in the garden now
Under my Mum's bluebell bush
But Flip and Flop they went somewhere else
Into the heaven that you flush
My dear old dog was thirteen years
When he was called to heel
And to this day I cannot say
Exactly how I feel
His bushy tail his black wet nose
To me he was so very clever
In my heart he will remain
Forever and ever and ever

Day Trips

They don't come around that often
Of that I can be sure
A day away from classroom
On to a castle or the shore
We get to wear our own clothes
With waterproofs in our rucksacks
The teachers also come dressed down
In their tracksuits and their slacks
We usually have a packed lunch
Which will be eaten in the rain
I'd much rather be somewhere abroad
Like France or Greece or Spain
By lunchtime we are all bored stiff
Of another battle won
I'd rather have my iPod on
Or just sit out in the sun
There is nothing that we've learned today
We couldn't have learned about in class
With Google and the Internet
We wouldn't have got a soggy ass
Do we really need to know this stuff
It's a real pain in the rear
But to get out of double Physics
We will do it every single year

Growing Up With Harry

I was a youngster when it started
And in my teens when the end came
I knew when I closed the final page
My life would never be the same

No more spells to cast or wands to wave
No more puzzles to work out
No more scars to heal or friends to save
No new tales to shout about

The dark lord got his just desserts
He was drained of all his luck
So come on Jo and write again
We want another book

Make-Up

Is there such a thing as too much
Perhaps at times there is
I think I have the balance right
Why does Dad get in a tizz

Just the right amount of lippy
Just the right amount of blush
Just the right amount of eye liner
Yet he still says it's too much

Just the right amount of mascara
Just enough eye shadow blend
Just the right amount of cover up
I borrowed from my friend

It makes me look much older
And covers up my spots
I don't think I could survive a day
Without my brushes creams and pots

He's a man he'll never understand
The things us girls go through
Some people call it make up
I call it beauty glue

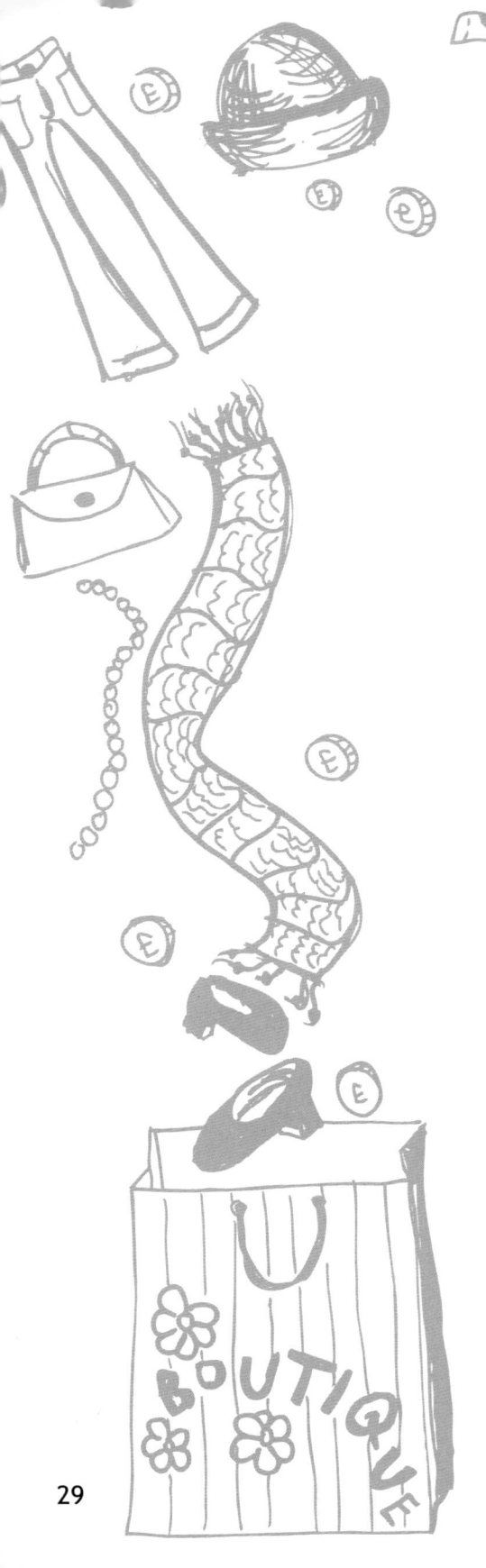

Fashion

These jeans they cost a fortune
Those heels were twice as much
That handbag that I saw last week
I wish was in my clutch

This skirt goes very well I'm told
With my old designer bag
It's the same one I saw an actress wear
In last weeks gossip mag

If I just shopped for clothes and shoes
In heaven I would be
Westwood Gucci Louboutin Dior
Lacroix and Versace

When I leave school I'll get a job
And end my fashion woes
Or maybe just marry a wealthy man
So I can afford designer clothes

Sleeping In

I have to check its Saturday
Why wake me up at eight
I've nothing to get up for
I'm not going to be late
My homework's done my room is clean
I cannot work it out
There is no school at all today
So why does my mother shout
Get up get dressed and clean your teeth
She says in dulcet tone

I need to check the time again
So I look up at my phone
I'm quite sure that it's the weekend
And in bed I'm gonna stay
I've nothing to get up for
I could lie in here all day
Oh no she started shouting again
This is not fair at all
Why can't I stay in bed I ask
She responds then with a call
Stay in bed all day she says
I couldn't care a less
I was going to take you shopping for
Some shoes and a new dress
Why didn't you say this first of all
Sleeping in's a waste of time
Cause missing out on a shopping trip
Now that really is a crime

Exams

Some people they start to get sweaty
Whilst others do not give a hoot
Some people are so nervous that they don't turn up
And others appear to go mute
When they tell us to turn over the paper
That's when the pressure on us all starts to mount
Some of us forget what our own names are
We forget how to spell and to count
Our palms they all start to get sticky
Our collars they all start to get tight
We question if we have got the answer wrong
Or if we have gotten it right
The teachers are just like our jailors
Walking up and then back down the isles
They make us sit in the exam chairs that long
I'm sure that it's giving me piles
I've filled in all of the answers
I thought I had finished but no
I take a look up at the school clock
And there is still over an hour to go
I check my exam paper then check it again
I think that my mind has gone blank
I then realise that I missed a full page
Oh no how my poor heart it sank
I scribble then draw and then scribble some more
Through the whole paper quickly I glance
Do I think that I've passed this particular exam
I think the answer is no feckin chance

Zits 3

There are ointments creams and different things
That will make them go away
But mine look like Vesuvius
I think they're here to stay

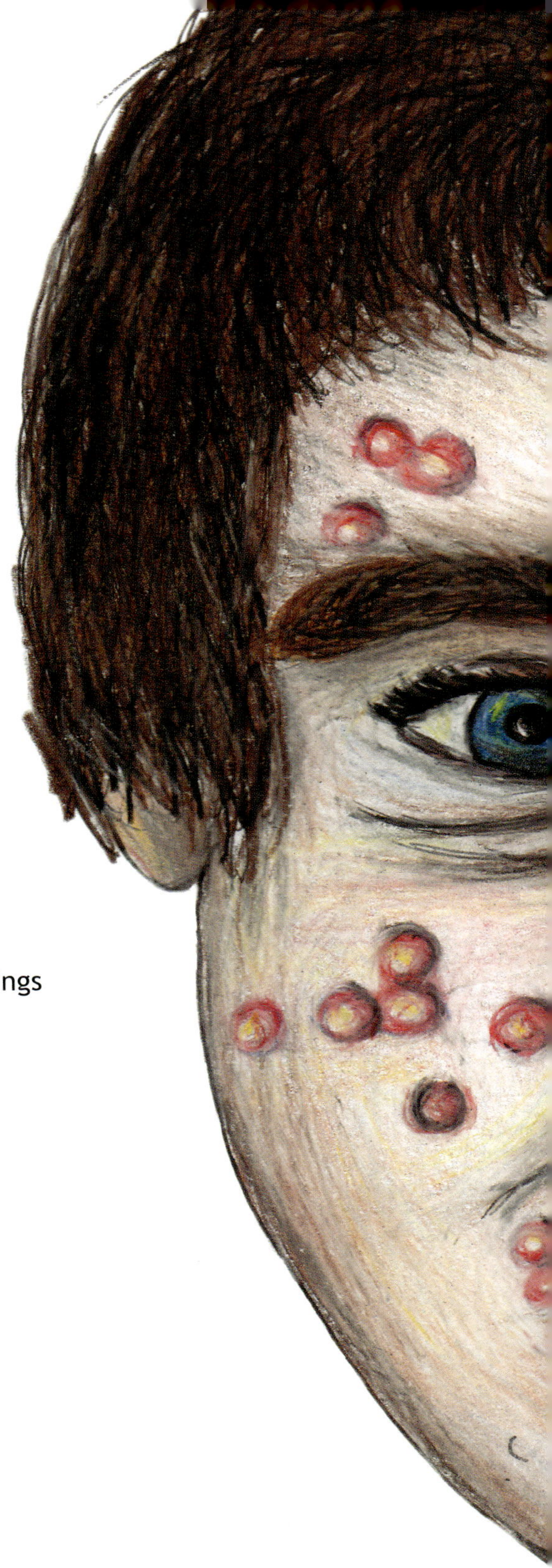

Mum

She wakes me in the morning
When I want to stay in bed
She makes me eat my breakfast
When I'm not ready to be fed
She makes me wash and brush my teeth
When I do not even smell
She knows if I'm not feeling well
When I can't even tell
She drops me off outside of school
When she's a million things to do
She knows if I am telling lies
When I say that it is true
She picks me up at 3.15
When school has let me go
She takes me home and cooks me food
When I play on Fifa Pro
She tells me when it's time for bed
When all my homeworks done
For all you do I'd like to say
Thank you
Your loving son

Dad

He is still in bed when I get up
I can hear him snore away
He makes noises that I can't repeat
I hear them everyday
He then gets up and drinks his tea
I watch him to the bathroom go
He then comes out and wafts his hands

I very nearly throw
He says to give it ten minutes more
I really wish he knew
He makes the bathroom smell just like
I am living in a zoo
He leaves his hair just everywhere
I feel embarrassed all the time
But even after all that stuff
I'm so glad my Dad is mine

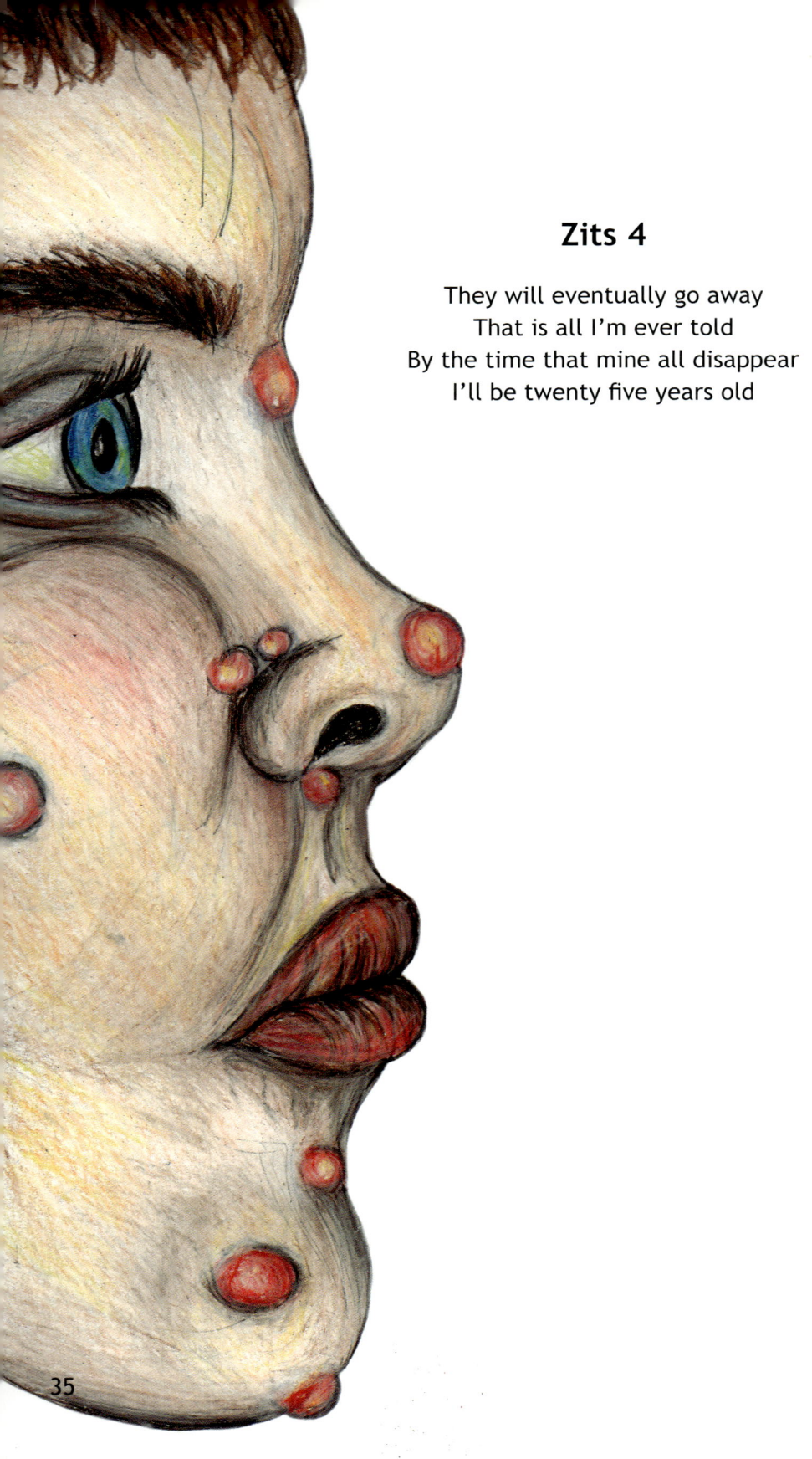

Zits 4

They will eventually go away
That is all I'm ever told
By the time that mine all disappear
I'll be twenty five years old

Pocket Money

My Dad always tells me his stories
Of way back when he was a lad
Of having to work for every penny he got
And all of the things that he never had
He tells me of never having a phone
I tell him that those days are gone
He tells me of all the records he's got
And the player that he plays them on
Way back when in the old days when he lived
He's convinced me of how it was so sad
But that's not my fault we have electricity now
And a few things that he wished he'd had
I can't remember how many times that I've heard
When he was my age how things were so bleak
But it's worth listening to all the old stories again
So I get my money at the end of the week

Holidays

The day has finally arrived
We're off to foreign shores
To sun and sand and two weeks off
From all my household chores
I'll probably spend most of my time
On the beach or by the pool
Put Ray-Ban's and my sun cream on
And play it rather cool

We have now arrived and I'm on the beach
There's a girl I like a bit
With her bikini and her golden skin
She's looking pretty fit
When she starts to rub the oil in
I'm sure she'll need a hand
I just wish that I could get up from
The small hole dug in the sand

Braces

They cling onto your teeth just like
A climber to a rock
I feel like everybody stares
And some of them will mock
They call me jaws and metal mouth
Also other kinds of names
I'm told my mouth looks just like
A track ridden on by trains
I get food caught in-between them
Which I get out with a pick
I can no longer chew on bubblegum
Nor toffee can I lick
The dentist told me two years
No more sweets or fizzy pop
All the things I like to nibble on
For now will have to stop

Leaving School

It only seems like yesterday
When I started at secondary school
I was told that I would get beaten up
And I wouldn't be able to follow the rules
I'll get my head flushed down the loo
By the bullies at least once a week
I wouldn't fit in with the jocks or cool kids
I'd be stuck in the back with the geeks
The homework would always be stressful
The teachers would always be mean
The corridors would be too busy for me
The school kitchen would never be clean
School dinners would always end up tasting like mush
Dinner ladies would always be rude
The older kids would line us all up
Give us wedgies then steal all our food
Our lessons would always be awful
My friends we would argue at times
I'd perhaps have a girlfriend or maybe a few
At times we'd be bored out of our minds
The time has now come for us to depart
After living through all of that strife
I must admit my old Dad was correct
They are the best days of your life

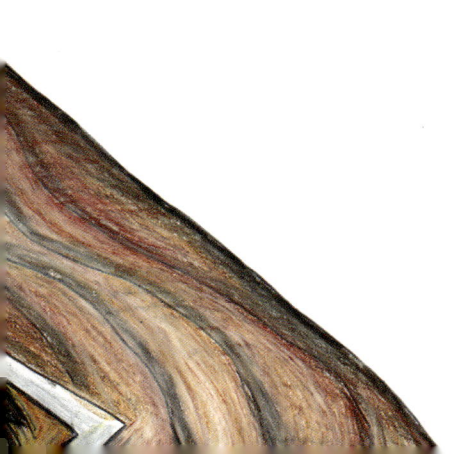

40

About the Author

Noel was born in Belfast in December 1970; I know. He doesn't look it. (Ed: He forced me to put that.) A self confessed failed actor and footballer, he now works as a speech writer and also writes sports reports for his local newspaper.

Noel's previous publications have been of a romantic nature, which, according to his wife, is as far away from his usually persona as you can get. He was inspired to write this book by his son who complained that there didn't appear to be any books of this nature for teenagers to read, so he asked his Dad to write one.

Noel currently lives in Lancashire, England with his long suffering wife and their two children.

About the Illustrator

Niamh is a visual communications graduate originating from the west coast of Ireland. After a few years working as a proper grown up in an office she decided to pursue her dream of being a starving artist (thankfully the starving part never came true) and spend a few years traipsing around the globe.

Niamh currently lives in Edinburgh with her husband Chris and spends time looking at pictures of cats, eating cheese and drawing pictures.

Niamh presently works as a freelance illustrator and graphic designer and is enjoying every odd project that comes her way